Get Close to Nature!

A Guessing Book

First published by Experience Early Learning Compa
7243 Scotchwood Lane, Grawn, Michigan 49637 U

Text Copyright © 2015 by Experience Early Learning Co.
Manufactured in No.8, Yin Li Street, Tian He District, Guangzhou,
Guangdong, China by Sun Fly Printing Limited
4th Printing 01/2023

ISBN: 978-1-937954-23-9
Visit us at www.ExperienceEarlyLearning.com

What am I?

I am a parrot!

Some types of parrots can live for over 80 years.

Parrots are one of the most intelligent types of birds and can even mimic human speech.

Parrots are omnivores, which means they eat both meat and plants. Most parrots eat a diet of nuts, seeds, flowers, fruit and insects.

I am a mushroom!

Mushrooms are made up of 90% water.

The thin, papery ribs under a mushroom's cap are called *gills*.

Over 30 types of mushrooms glow in the dark. The glow attracts insects that spread its spores.

I am a turtle!

A turtle's shell is attached to its body.
It gets bigger as the turtle grows.

Most turtles can hide their head and legs
inside their shells if predators attack.

Turtles have nerve endings in their shells.
If you touch its shell, a turtle can feel it.

What am I?

I am a sunflower!

Sunflowers can grow 8-12 feet tall in just 6 months.

The head of a sunflower is actually made up of many tiny flowers called florets.

One sunflower can have as many as 2,000 seeds.

I am a fish!

Most fish have taste buds all over their body.

As a fish grows, its scales increase in size. In this way, growth rings are formed that reveal the age of a fish.

Fish scales are usually covered with a layer of slime that helps the fish move smoothly through the water.

What am I?

I am a worm!

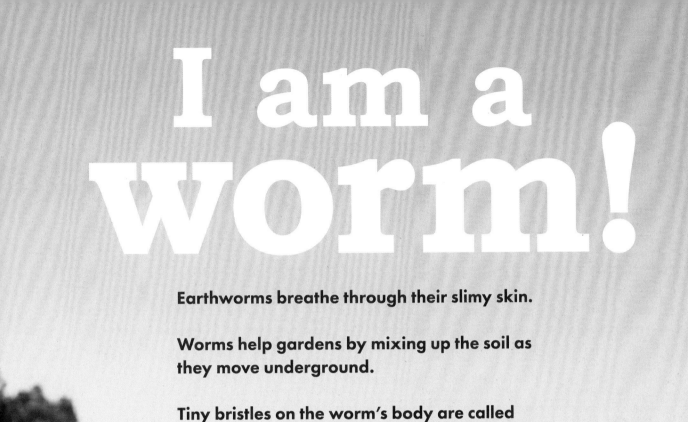

Earthworms breathe through their slimy skin.

Worms help gardens by mixing up the soil as they move underground.

Tiny bristles on the worm's body are called *setae*. They help the worm move through soil.

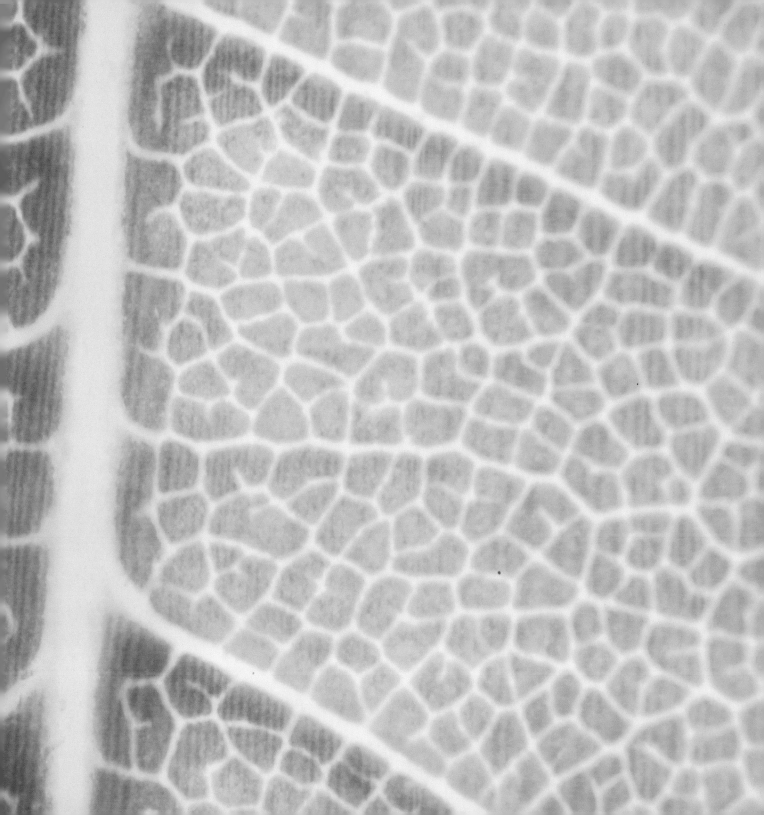

I am a leaf!

Leaves are the food factories of a plant where energy is converted into sugar.

The veins in a leaf support it and carry food and water to the plant or tree.

All plants contain *chlorophyll*, a chemical that gives them their green color.

What am I?

I am a butterfly!

Butterflies have taste receptors on their feet.

Butterflies have 4 wings with unique patterns
made up of tiny scales.

The wing patterns warn predators of danger
and help the butterfly blend into its surroundings.

What am I?

I am a lotus!

Lotus flowers can be white or pink, and they grow in shallow, murky waters.

The lotus flower is known for its pleasing scent.

Various parts of the lotus flower can be eaten or used to make teas or medicines.

What am I?

I am a tree!

Trees provide a home for all sorts of animals.

Bark is the outside layer of the tree that protects the more delicate layers of wood underneath.

Water and nutrients travel from the roots, up the trunk, through the branches and all the way to the leaves.

Fun Facts!

Parrots - Some parrot species can live for over 80 years.

Mushrooms - There are over 30 species of mushrooms that actually glow in the dark.

Turtles - Just like your bones, a turtle's shell is actually part of its skeleton.

Sunflowers - The world's tallest sunflower reached 30 feet and 1 inch.

Fish - The largest fish is the whale shark. It can grow to 50 feet long.

Worms - In one acre of land, there can be more than a million earthworms.

Butterflies - Butterflies use their feet to taste.

Lotus - Lotus plants can survive thousands of years.

Trees - The General Sherman Tree is the largest living tree in the world. It stands 275 feet tall.